MW00770844

KEYS TO A WOMAN'S HEART

Written by

Antonio Simpson

VMH Vikki M. Hankins™ Publishing
3355 Lenox Rd. NE Suite 750 Atlanta, GA 30326
www.vmhpublishing.com

Manufactured in the United States of America

Hardback ISBN: 978-1-947928-15-2

10 9 8 7 6 5 4 3 2 1

Book Cover Design: VMH Publishing
Front Book Cover Image: Shutterstock
Back Cover/Flap Photographer: Trent Lawrence
ptmphotography

Publisher's Note:

Special thanks to:

Katrina Holt – Mother
Angelo Simpson– Twin Brother, Best Friend
VMH Publishing
Chiquita Sheppard (ex wife) – The Inspiration
Behind the Book
Qiana Cannon – Sister
Brookhaven Boys and Girls Club – Atlanta GA
Voorhees College
Cross KEYS High School – Atlanta GA

Introduction

To Whom It May Concern:

If you are holding this book, it's because deep in your heart you are yearning for more in your relationship. Perhaps your marriage is drifting apart and you are confused about what the problem may be.

As a man, I can say that most of us have done very well in our careers. We have worked so hard to build a successful career, achieve success in our business, and obtain a better financial life for ourselves. However, a lot of us still fail to attain the same success in our relationships and marriages.

We do not realize how some of our actions and inactions tend to destroy our marriages and affect the woman we love. When the problems become uncontrollable, we blame our partner, failing to acknowledge our mistakes and take responsibility for our actions.

It is true that a woman usually determines whether or not a marriage lasts a lifetime. However, how you treat your partner and what you put in determines what you get. Clint Eastwood observed, "What you put into life is what you get out of it."

Unfortunately, many men tend to care more about what their relationship offers them than how much effort they put into it. When their relationships fall apart, they justify their failures.

A man in a relationship is what a foundation is to an erected house. If a house is built upon a weak foundation it collapses, but when built upon a firm foundation, it tends to last almost a lifetime.

Is your relationship shaking? Is your marriage drifting apart? Are you treated by misfortune in your marriage? It could be that you are not being the best person you can be. It is essential that all of us think about our lives and ask ourselves what we truly want in our relationship. How much have we put in? How often have we tried to be the man we think our partner deserves? What must we do to become better? Socrates remarked, "An unexamined life is not worth living." It is important that we examine ourselves and work towards building a successful relationship with our partner.

How can I lead my marriage and relationship towards success?

This remains the right question. To find out how you can become a better man to your partner, I suggest that you do the following:

- Read each chapter to better understand what your partner really needs from you.

- Evaluate yourself at the end of each chapter by answering the performance question.

- Take the action steps included to implement the kind of qualities described in the chapter.

THE PAINFUL TRUTH . . .

If you were given a chance to change just one thing in your life, what would that be?

My marriage ended ten months after I wedded my ex-wife. She is the most beautiful lady I have ever seen and losing her was my biggest regret. I failed her as a man. But how could I have known? I didn't realize then how my behavior and actions affected our marriage.

It hurts my pride to say that I was an immature man and failed to understand that it was also my responsibility to build up my marriage and family. I was inconsistent and failed to properly communicate with her because I feared the new responsibility at hand; I subconsciously forced her to take the lead. She tried to communicate to me, but I was too busy to listen, too proud to understand. I let her down.

So many men today have made terrible mistakes like I did in their relationships, and some others continue to make even more. Until we acknowledge these mistakes we may never get it right.

I know my mistakes now, but unfortunately it is already too late. But you still have a chance to make it right, to build yourself up and become the man your marriage needs. Become her greatest motivator and inspirer. This is your chance to build a happy home with your partner where your children will grow knowing that they are not alone.

Acknowledge your mistakes, assess yourself, and learn how you can become better. Get to work, it begins with a single decision; I hope you make the right one.

Chapter 1

Make Her a Priority

Until February 2017, I took my marriage for granted. I had been married to her for just ten months. I take responsibility for our failed marriage because now I realize how my behavior and what I thought I knew affected my marriage. Believe me, she was a wonderful woman, but I was ignorant of my actions. The truth is, I cared more about myself. I took my career more seriously than my wife and failed to be there for her when she needed me. Now, I understand why my marriage was unsuccessful.

Oftentimes, we neglect the things which matters most in our lives. We neglect our families, our partner, our marriages and relationships. We think more about ourselves. We grow more concerned about what we want and we fail to acknowledge the real meaning of love. But if our families, our relationships, and our marriages are established upon love, then we have to learn to express that love in full.

For a marriage to be successful, it requires two unconditional lovers who are committed to outdoing each other in acts of sacrificial giving, selfless serving, undeserved forgiveness, unreserved admiration, heartfelt compassion and willful submission. This means that you have to make your partner and marriage a priority in your life.

What does a woman want?

Women are quite different from men in their ways of thinking. Men are rational and women are feelers. Men work by cause and effect, but women work and make decisions based on what they feel.

It may sound true that women are the most complicated species, but it is also true that they have the simplest nature. The saying "The simplest things are often the most difficult" backs up this fact.

Most of the time, women will not directly tell you what they want from you. They imply it with their body language or actions, and expect you to understand and act upon that message.

Most men focus more on the outward appearance than the inside. They think that working each day to provide their partner with money, food, clothes, and a spa treatment is enough to make her happy. They are often disappointed when the opposite occurs.

Yes, you must work and yes, you should be able to take care of most of her needs. But in your relationship and marriage, what a woman really wants is the simple things that are often overlooked, such as spending as much time as you do money with her, calling her from work to know how she's doing, playing with her and having a casual discussion, instead of always talking about work, and spending a Friday evening with her instead of always working late hours.

Women love to be flattered. Calling them romantic names and singing praises to them gives them great joy. It gives women the feeling that you adore and appreciate them. Some men never flatter their wives, unless they are asked. They can never tell their wife or girlfriend how beautiful she is or how sexy and adorable they think she is.

Women love to feel special in the eyes of their man. They want their man to make them feel like the only woman in the world. They want to know that you are always thinking about them most of the time. Some men never care to reassure their wives of her importance in their life. They go with the thought that she knows. The truth is that a woman wants to hear her man tell her how important she is to him and how serious he takes their relationship.

A woman also loves to hear her man tell her that he loves her and how much he loves the relationship even when they know he does. Most men do not say this to their partner

often and some men never say it at all.
Telling your partner the three golden words
makes her feel comfortable and secure in the
relationship.

A simple call from work or anywhere else
creates a significant impression in a
relationship. Sparing a few seconds or
minutes of your time to say "Hello"
unconsciously creates a significant
impression in a woman's conscious mind.

Some men are too busy to call their partner
to say "Hi" and some men never care. To
them, it isn't necessary, since she was okay
when he left for work. By acting this way,
you subconsciously create a crack in your
relationship.

Tasks as simple as calling home from work
and planning a dinner with your wife or
girlfriend can be all your relationship needs
to improve.

Some men are fond of missing a well
planned romantic dinner with their wife.

Nothing dejects a woman like the disappointment.

It is true that no human is entirely alike. Therefore, it is very important to note that not everything a woman wants is highlighted in this chapter. Men differ in their wants and needs, so do women. It is advised that you try to find out from your partner what she expects from you and work harder to be that man. If you have everything she wants, I must say kudos.

Chapter 2

Be Consistent

Consistency means always being there for her, showing her that you care and reaffirming that you love her no matter the situation. Consistency means never changing or more preferably, always improving; Not having conflicting identities —caring today and acting like you don't care tomorrow or loving her today and the next day it's a whole new unattractive you.

Some men are in a way, what I call consistently inconsistent. They behave in the same manner like a light switch—frequently on and off in their relationship. They are there today and the next day, they disappear. They are not consistent in their interactions, both in behavior and communication. They are always putting up mixed emotions that leave their partner wondering, "Is he still interested or not?" They are not always present in the relationship—physically, emotionally, or psychologically.

They will call you today to check on you, to say hello, and to tell you that they truly love you. They will text you and send you romantic text messages that would blow your mind and make you fall deeper in love with them. They come around and take you out for a romantic dinner, hang out with you, take you to the beach. But then, after a few days, they are off. They won't call or text you. They won't check on you and this particular off-behavior goes on for days and adds emotional stress. You wonder what may have happened and if they're okay. You can hear your heart racing and you lose sleep, only to find out days after that he's okay and isn't really busy, but just didn't feel like coming around.

Some men are fond of going cold when the weather seems unfavorable. They act hot if the relationship is moving interestingly, but when unfavorable circumstances arise—

when misunderstandings come up between them, they run off. They go into the dark leaving their partner all alone and emotionally disturbed.

This sarcastic behavior makes your partner feel unsure of what your true intentions and feelings are, keeping her on the edge and the relationship undefined. It leaves her with questions of, "What is wrong? Is he no longer interested in us? Does he want to break up? Did I do something wrong? Is he seeing someone else?" You can perceive the emotional instability and insecurity which is the main initiator of break-ups and divorces.

We most often, foolishly take pride in our inconsistent attitude—proudly asking, "Why would our partner accuse us of seeing someone else?"

But then you would have to ask yourself again, "Why wouldn't she?" If you were in her shoes, would you not think the same?

Consistency in a relationship shows seriousness. It means that you're dedicated to building a happy and successful relationship with your partner. It makes your partner feel confident that you love her just as you said, and that your relationship means as much to you as it does to her.

It's relatable to your place of work. You love your job and you don't want to lose it. You'll agree with me that you always make sure you get to work early every working day, that you're dedicated to your job because it means so much to you, and even when you're stressed out or feel uncomfortable and wish you could leave work to rest, you don't. You find strength within you and off you go.

That's consistency—the mark of seriousness and dedication, and that's exactly what your relationship needs too. To be diligent and dedicated, no matter the circumstances.

Understandably, odd circumstances like past unsuccessful relationships or your fanatic way of playing women may have turned you into behaving the way you do now. No matter what may be the reason, it isn't enough to justify your inconsiderate behavior in your present relationship.

Look at your present relationship. Think about your current partner and ask yourself questions concerning your unlovely attitude. Does she take me seriously? Does she put more effort to make this relationship work? Does she love me and show it? Am I treating her right like I should or am I letting my past experience affect us now?

This is where people get it wrong. They allow their hurtful past relationship experiences control how they behave in the present. They find it very difficult to let go of the hurt and end up unintentionally hurting someone else too. Frankly, that doesn't make you feel any better, but instead, you lose your real chance of finding a true partner and having a better relationship.

You can end up feeling heartbroken after because of your past unsuccessful relationship, but the undeniable truth is that if you learn to move on and open your heart to new experiences and possibilities, five years, ten years, twenty years later, you will look back and be thankful to whoever broke your heart. If she never did, you wouldn't have been married to your current wife who is extraordinarily amazing or your girlfriend who loves you unconditionally.

Building security in the *us* relationship is all about building trust, and the only way one can build trust is being consistent. Trust is essential for a successful relationship. When we trust our spouses, we are able to give freely to them and to the relationship because we believe that our spouse would reliably and responsibly give us and the relationship what it needs. Trust builds a sense of security and prevents the relationship from drifting into suspicion and instability. It also allows the relationship to develop a deeper intimacy.

Consistency and trust allows us to accomplish two key things in our relationship. First, it allows us to rely on the fact that our marital relationship will continue. It is the foundation for knowing that we are not alone and that we can experience a compassionate love for one another. Second, it allows us to predict how the spouse and the relationship would behave. Although we cannot rely on the past, past experiences give us a clue of how we can relate in the future. For instance, in the company or firm where you work, if you have been told by your employer that you'll be paid at the end of each month and have received your paychecks at exactly the same date for years, you can confidently predict that you will continue to receive your paycheck on the same date at the end of each month. Because of this, you plan your expenditures accordingly. Now, you can see the importance of consistency. When your partner can predict how her spouse and relationship will behave, she can make sure that her behavior suits the expectations of her spouse, and you can work to fit with hers. This way, both of you can work for the success of the relationship.

The good news is that no matter how complicated a relationship can be or how difficult the problems in it may seem, consistency can provide a happy and successful relationship if you make it a habit. The more you engage in a consistent behavior, the more solid your relationship will become. Spoil her with consistency.

Chapter 3

Learn To Spend Quality Time With Your Partner

Some men think dating is only necessary when they're ready to find a mate. They think that dating when you're married is a waste of time and money especially if kids are involved.

I guess you're thinking "I don't have time. I already have more than I can handle. The kids have school. My job takes every minute of my time. My parents are getting older and require extra care. My job requires at least one week of travel per month. I'm so tired I can barely see straight—and you're asking me to add a date night to my endless lists of responsibilities?"

But the truth is, if you want to keep your relationship alive and growing, you have to date your partner.

A marriage without fun is like a bird without wings—it suffers and dies.

Women have a natural spark within them. They love to have fun and they sure know how to get it. When a woman gets married and somehow loses that spark, she eventually becomes frustrated. She feels unattractive and her worth diminishes. Sometimes when it goes overboard, she gets unnecessarily angry or aggressive and you may begin to wonder what's come over her. You have.

Your life may have changed a little bit now that you're married to her, but your blueprint hasn't. You don't have to drop your responsibilities like everything has changed, and pretend your work doesn't matter anymore.

Yes, you may achieve financial stability, successfully raise your children, and guide them through school. But when you reach the empty nest years, you realize that you've been a stranger to your wife all along.

Cultivate the habit of dating. Or rather, reignite it. The habit of dating is the catalyst for building your relationship and staying emotionally connected through the coming years.

Spending uninterrupted quality time with your partner is a great recipe for a successful relationship and marriage. A healthy relationship with an intimate partner requires nurturing and attention. There are no quick fixes or fast-track methods to obtain satisfaction and happiness in a long-term relationship.

You are busy, you don't have that time. You've got better things to do with your money. But when your marriage begins to crumble and you end up visiting a therapist, you will realize that you've just spent the same amount or even more time and money trying to fix your marriage. Prevention is far better than the cure.

As engaging as your week can be, you can still spend the weekend or an evening with your partner. Your time does not control you, you create and control it. And if you understand that your marriage or relationship is as important as your job, if not more, then will you create time to spend with your partner.

Remember the things you did to make her fall in love with you are the things you must do to keep her in love with you, whether you are long married with six children or in your fifties.

You might be wondering right now, how can committing to regular date nights revolutionize your marriage or relationship?

> *Date nights rekindle the romance in your relationship.* Having a night out with your partner is a very important part of blazing your romance.

Date nights strengthen your commitment. By engaging in regular date nights, you communicate to your partner that you are committed to strengthening your marriage by spending ongoing quality time together.

Date nights strengthen your bond. The more time you spend alone enjoying each other, the closer and stronger your bond becomes. This naturally deepens your intimacy.

Date nights inject excitement into your stale marriage. You've got a lot of stress from work, childrearing, and some other issues you tend to, and because you no longer have that time, your marriage has become boring and unpleasant. You could have a date with your partner, where you both talk about the things you used to love. Visit places, go to the movies. Do some little crazy things together. Bring back the laughter, the fun, which in turn energizes you to face your mundane daily routine.

It's not enough to talk about having a date with your wife, you must actually have a proper date with your partner.

Making your partner feel distress in the middle of the date is as worse as not having a date at all.

It's so dissatisfying how chivalry has gone. Some men no longer think it wise to treat their lady special with gentle respect. They think it's all old-fashioned now to open the car door or restaurant door for their partner. They think now that they're being too gentle when they pull out the chair for her to sit in.

There is nothing more romantic to a woman than when her man treats her like a queen and there is nothing more disrespectful than when she's treated so manly.

Keys to a Woman's Heart

Chapter 4

Men at Work - Being a Leader

I guess the first thing that popped into your head when you saw the theme of this chapter was the Australian rock band that came to prominence in the 1980s. But no, I'm talking about a very important factor: **Responsibility.**

Maturity is not evident by your age, but by your fruit—your sense of responsibility. I have learned that growing up is natural; there's nothing we can do to slow down time, you are older now than you were when you first picked up this book. And you're even older now. And now. And now. You see what I mean? However, you can be immature forever. Growing up and becoming a responsible man is to be classified as mature; not just a person that's full of years.

The sense of responsibility is a rare gift available only to those who strive for it. Ezra Taft Benson said, "The responsibility of a man is to lead his family. Men understand this law in the natural world, and work with it, but few understand it in a mental and moral world and they, therefore, do not cooperate with it."

The very alarming thing about so many marriages today is the way people jump in and out of them. Frankly, some people don't know what they are walking into, and unexpected circumstances send them running.

It's very tragic when men try to escape from their duty to provide. Now, thousands of men walk away from their family responsibilities. They are not only lazy men with no initiative but among them are men who have lost their sense of dignity.

Some men assume the position of a couch in their home and ignorantly shy away from their responsibilities as the leader of their home, which is to provide for their family, and to a greater extent, take pride in that.

These kind of men have one thing in common - excuses. If there is anything they do so well, it is make excuses for their incompetence and failure. They often blame others or even the country for their inability to work hard and earn, so as to provide for the material needs of their family.

I have heard some men blame their parents for their own failure. Some too, blame the hard situation of their country as the reason for their inability to become responsible enough. This boils down to one thing - attitude. Hans Selye said "Adopting the right attitude can convert a negative stress into a positive one." This means that, though the situation of your country may be unfavorable, or you may come from a poor background, if you will it, you can win.

The right sense of responsibility is an offspring of maturity. A woman admires a man who takes full responsibility for his duties towards his family, and this means taking responsibility for your actions, your decisions and your reactions. Until a man begins to take responsibility for these, only then can he be respected by his wife.

Actions speak louder than words as we all know. A woman does not admire a man who just talks about his dreams and plans, but a man who takes action by working towards them.

It is the man's responsibility to provide for his family. Providing for one's family is not all drudgery and pain. Yes, leading and providing for the family is the hardest job a man can ever have, but a man in himself has been endowed with all the potential he needs to ascend to that position. One of the responsibilities of a husband is to provide materially for the family. The material needs include food and clothing.

The worthy man recognizes and accepts the responsibility of provision, which is actually the least of the three essential needs of every family.

The second responsibility of a total man is in the area of emotional security. A man needs to understand that his wife and children need to feel safe, cared for, and worthy of his time. Unfortunately, all of the financial and material provisions cannot make up for the emotional damages that occur when these are missing. As a woman, and from my experience with my clients, I would say that the most urgent need a woman requires is security. A man is responsible for providing the sense of security for his wife and children.

Security does not rely on a huge salary, beautiful house, and luxuries. Some men are fond of creating emotional alertness with their wives. They do not care about surrounding themselves with ladies and how that singular act could produce a doubt of their faithfulness in the heart of their wife. Women tell me, "I don't need the best of everything; what I really want is my husband. I want him to share his life with me." Security gives the woman the assurance that you won't abandon her. It is this security that inspires her to trust in you. And be assured that nothing substitutes for security in a woman's life.

The next responsibility of a man is to express love and affection. I cannot explain in depth how one can express affection. The simplest ways to show affection is by look and touch. Do you remember when you first saw her? How in one glance, you transmitted the whole message to her? If you have forgotten or have not learned to express your affection for your wife through a loving glance, it would benefit you to learn.

Touch is an extension of the real you. How often do you caress your wife in ways that convey affection without demanding more from her?

Your verbal expression also is so much more important. How often do you tell your wife that you love her and that you think she's the greatest and the most amazing woman in the world? The same applies to your children.

Is there any woman who does not like to be told that she is truly beautiful? Like I said is the previous chapters, every woman loves to receive flattery from her husband often. Wouldn't she love you dearly if she felt very special in your arms?

Another responsibility of a man is understanding. Understanding is a very vital key to a successful marriage. It is said that women are impossible to be understood. That's because men are not women. Understanding means that you accept her just as she is and you are not continually trying to make her someone else. Understanding is a duty a man owes his wife and it is his duty to know her, recognize how she reacts to different situations, empathize with her struggles, appreciate her strengths, respond with compassion to her areas of weakness, and listen carefully to what she tells you. That is understanding.

How do I react to situations? How effective are my decisions? Do I apply wisdom? What line of actions do I take after I've made decisions? These are very important questions every man needs to ask himself. I will say this to you- look into your heart. It tells the story of why you were made.

Leadership itself a far more complex virtue that most men don't have. Often times, men jump into marriage without realizing that they have the responsibility to lead their wife and household.

I call them the weak men. They lack integrity. They can't face challenges. They cannot take the first move. They are indecisive because they fear that they may fail. Personally, they do not know what they want in life. They are always afraid to take the first step. Their reactions to unpleasant situations are rather odious.

Like John C. Maxwell rightly said, "A leader is one who knows the way, goes the way, and shows the way."

Women admire great men who aren't afraid to make decisions and take action. They admire men who aren't afraid to face challenges.

Do you know why women are attracted to men in leadership positions? The popular misconception that men have is that those men earn approximately $30,000 dollars more per month than the average worker.

But the truth is that it has nothing to do with how much they earn, but the characteristics that this position implies:

- *The ability to make decision*

- *The power to inspire and motivate*

- *The emotional strength to lead*

The responsibilities of these persons in position are not different from that of a husband to his wife and family. And as such, should possess the same characteristics. What you do from this moment determines the sustenance of your relationship and marriage. I'll end this chapter with quotes from great achievers.

- "The responsibility of a man is to lead his family." *(Ezra Taft Benson)*

- "A good leader knows the way, goes the way, and shows the way." *(John C. Maxwell)*

- "Having family responsibilities and concerns just has to make you more understanding person." *(Sandra Day O'Connor)*

- "If you don't like a situation, change it. If you can't change it, change your attitude." *(Maya Angelou)*

- "Family responsibility, yes, and always. Family bankruptcy due to the cruel rules of government, no." *(Barbara Mikulski)*

Keys to a Woman's Heart

Chapter 5

Let Go of Your Pride

C. S. Lewis, a scholar and the author of *The Chronicles of Narnia*, remarked, "Pride is spiritual cancer: It eats up the possibility of love, or contentment or even common sense." It is often accompanied by a big ego.

Most families today are built by men whose pride rules them. No one is like them and no one and nothing is ever good enough for them. They love to be praised and worshipped like some god.

Pride is recorded as the deadliest amongst the seven deadly sins of nature that blinds one's eyes to see his faults and to become great. It is a spirit of sarcasm that tells you, you're great when it actually means you're not.

Pride today has left so many marriages shattered and many relationships inadequate.

Men of pride and ego have turned themselves into gods and their partner their footstool. And the one question we are left with is, why?

Pride always goes with his accomplices, like ignorance, anger, self-centeredness, desperation, deviousness, you name them. It clouds your judgment, it tells you that you're always right and there is no other like you. It makes you ignorant of other people's presence and feelings. It tells you that you're the master and you are not bound by any rules and everyone must follow your own rules.

At that note, I ask you, "What are you that someone else hasn't been? What have you achieved or possess that no one else has? The one thing more difficult to overcome than an addiction is pride. It blinds your eyes from seeing your own faults, it shuts your ears from hearing other people's opinions and advice and kills the heart so you cannot feel.

This is you:

1. EGO

Because you earn more than your partner does or you came from a very wealthy family and she didn't, you have no respect for her. You act however you feel and you do not think she has the right to tell you what to do.

2. FAULT-FINDER

You are a fault-finder, a critic. Nothing she does pleases you. You always complain at everything. No matter how hard she tries, you always find a fault and instead of appreciating her effort, you bark at her like a mad dog.

3. SUPERIORITY

You always see yourself as the alpha and the omega. No one ever questions your actions and decisions. When she does, you rage at her, beating her up. You believe no one knows but you and because of that, only your decisions and opinions are right.

4. CONTROLLING

You want to be in control all the time. You want your partner and your children to submit to you. It's you to decide where they go, who the make friends with, and what they do.

5. SELF-CENTERED

You are very self-centered. No one else matters. You do not care about other people's feelings. You don't care about your partner's needs (both emotional and material), her struggles and her feelings. You lack a sense of humor. All that matters is yourself and what you need. And when it seems like you're not getting it the way you wanted, you go repulsive and don't mind fighting her.

6. ABUSIVE

Your pride has turned you into an abusive man. You are always quick to voice very disrespectful and scornful words to your partner at every little mistake. You do not mind embarrassing her in front of your friends or in public.

7. SELF-PRAISE

There is none like you. You tell yourself how great you are and that you deserve to be honored by others. You are used to telling your partner that she doesn't deserve you and she should be grateful you picked her.

8. EMPATHY

You have gone cold and unaware of your children's needs. You don't show concern for them as a good father should. You are never a part of your children's lives and you don't think there is anything wrong with it.

9. LIES

What makes you worse than any other type of liar is, not only do you lie to others, you lie more to yourself. You tell yourself that you're good and you know it all, but in all honesty, you don't.

10. IRRESPONSIBLE

Since you never make mistakes, you are very good at blaming others for your own incompetence. You never take the responsibility for your actions and decisions even when you make all of them.

A proud-hearted man shows off not just in his home, but everywhere else—like in his workplace around his colleagues and friends. A proud-hearted man is always too quick to anger. You place yourself above others and when you feel that you're not receiving the honor you think you deserve, you feel belittled and you become aggressive.

Pride and ego destroy relationships, marriages, and friendship faster than any other vice. It prevents your ability to be a great partner to your spouse, a better friend, and a greater father to your children. Henry cloud advised, *"Leave your pride, ego, and narcissism somewhere else. Reactions from these parts of you will reinforce your children's most primitive fears."*

It takes away love, trust, happiness, friendship, intimacy, empathy, deep connection, understanding . . . and without these very important qualities, a relationship is dead.

An apostolate, G. Maura remarked, *"The closest to death is pride: it closes your eyes so you can't see your own mistakes. It shuts your hears from hearing others' opinions. It clouds your mind and prevents it from reasoning properly. It infects your brain and loses your sense of responsibility. It consumes your heart and makes it impossible to feel love and happiness— leaving you half-dead."*

Unfortunately, it may be difficult to realize and acknowledge the pride and ego in you because it has possessed your mind to think otherwise. Everyone can't be wrong at the same time. You partner and friends may have told you of your ill-attitude very many times and if they have, then it's time to think for a change.

To take control of your pride can be very difficult, but it's as possible too. You may ask now, how you can overcome your pride. To overcome your pride, you must first, acknowledge it and that may be the only thing you have to do.

Acknowledging your pride is not as easy as it sounds because it has blocked your mind from ever thinking that you are one. But take few moments to discuss and listen to your partner and friends. Let them tell you what they think and how they truly feel about your ego and that will tell you more.

Chapter 6

Learn to Control Your Anger

Anger!

Regrettably, it has ended so many relationships and marriages and has left many lives miserable. So many men have lost their relationships, their partner, their family and even their children because of their rage. It has taken so many lives to the grave and continues to.

You know the feeling too. When you've lost many relationships and a partner who loved you. How you hit your wife and stole her freedom. How your children fear you now like you're a monster. How you are going through a divorce right now and she tells you, it's your entire fault.

It scares you too, you know that. You're frustrated and maybe you don't know what to do about it. You've tried to control it but it's not working. Maybe it's not your intention to always have angry outburst, but no one understands how you really feel. Or maybe you don't understand what's going on yourself.

It is a very sad feeling. It often ends with regrets for the harm we may have caused at any point in time. Sometimes we end up doing something permanently stupid. Sometimes too, we lose those we truly love because we were temporarily upset. Anger doesn't make us stronger but shows us how weak we are inside. It tells us that we are good enough. We are the real victims, not those we pour it out on.

Sadly, very many men are almost alike. Few of them don't understand what the real problem is. Some do try to fight it within themselves alone and the more they try, the more their anger grips them. And until you recognize and acknowledge where it came from and how it all began, you may never overcome it.

Uncontrollable anger is an outcome of unpleasant, continuous events or experiences that have built up in a person's life over time, affecting their psychology. It's more of a psychological problem than the circumstances you're reacting to. But unfortunately, because your partner reacts to your anger in the same manner, you become angrier and eventually do things you later regret.

In order to learn to control your anger, you first must understand why you're angry. Are you angry because your partner receives calls from other men or are you angry because you feel that you're not good enough for her so you fear that she may dump you for another man?

Are you angry because you asked her for some assistance and she couldn't help you or are you angry because her not helping you made you feel like you don't deserve to be assisted? Maybe you feel rejected by her because all of your life, you have been ignored by those close relatives you've asked for assistance from.

These experiences have in some way affected you very negatively. The continuous occurrences have made you feel not good enough and in time made you hate yourself. So whenever similar situations happen, it reminds you of what you fear the most and the only way you express your emotions is through anger.

As anger increases, one's perceptive becomes narrow. Uncontrollable anger is really a form of tunnel vision. One's thoughts become centered on injury and attack; their reasoning is impaired and they act and say things that seem crazy once they are calm again.

SELF-HATE

Extreme anger is a built-up feeling stemming from past experiences and circumstances in a person's life, like multiple rejections or childhood trauma.

There are several reasons why you would hate yourself. Your past experiences have made you feel that you aren't good enough. You've had several unsuccessful relationships. You gave your best and had loved genuinely, but they all end up leaving you without saying a word about it, and maybe they've told you, you aren't the kind of man they need. It made you feel very hurt and rejected. You wonder why they leave and question if there is something wrong with you because they just keep leaving. You eventually feel used and you accept that there must be something wrong with you that makes them all disappear.

You eventually end up hating yourself. The feeling that you are not good enough has eaten you deeply and has affected your psychology. It took you a long time, maybe years before finding a new relationship. And all those years, you've been alone. You have kept your problems to yourself and tried to fight it alone, but the more you tried to fight it, the deeper the feeling.

Now you tell yourself, you are not good enough. Finally, you are in a new relationship, but you fear it may end like just like the previous ones. You can't let yourself be used again. So you start acting overprotective. Every time you sense the same feeling, you become uncontrollably angry. Every time even a minor misunderstanding arises between you and your partner, you get a grip that she may leave you like always and you express your sad fears by getting uncontrollably angry.

Every time you see her talking to another man or go through her cell phone, you unconsciously perceive that she wants to leave you and you get even more angry. Because you don't want to get hurt again, you ban her from talking to other men. You try to control where she goes and what she does. You do not wish to do these things, but you can't help it, you don't want to get hurt again, understandably.

But you are getting it all wrong. You know it has not made your relationship any better. By acting in such manner, you will only end up driving her into the arms of another man and you will eventually feel used again.

The young man described above got very angry at his partner not because she couldn't give him what he needed at the time he needed it, but really because he felt undeserving. This is another form of self-hate which builds anger in people. Its often begins from childhood.

You've never got anything you asked for especially from your parent(s). In your household, you were the only one who was never given what you wanted most of the time, and those times you were given something, you were scolded before having it. Every one of your siblings got what they asked for, but you. It made you feel rejected and not worthy enough to have anything—a self-hate. And it continued up until you grew into an adult. This experience has made you hate who you are and it eventually resulted in you not being able to love someone else deeply too.

Anger became the only way you knew how to best express your emotions. You hate the feeling, you hate yourself and you hate to be told, "No" or "Later." Sometimes others see you as ungrateful or in some cases, disrespectful, and that makes you even angrier. Every time your partner tells you, "No," you feel undeserving of what you have asked from her and it provokes you over again.

You're always too quick to anger and you tend to lose more control every time. But this feeling always ends with regret. Most of the time in your relationship, it's more fights than peace and you can feel your relationship drifting apart.

But you cannot continue to see yourself as undeserving. To love your partner deeply, you must first love yourself. You cannot overcome it alone. You have to communicate to your partner what the actual problem is and work together to rebuilding your self-worth and loving yourself again. You deserve so much more than you think and the truth is, if she never thought you to be worthy of her love, she would haven't fallen for you. Think about it, before you two interacted, she had met more than a million men and no one was able to steal her heart, but you.

You may have been hurt several times before, but you cannot let it torment you. You have to move on no matter how difficult it may seem. You have to open your heart to your partner and learn to trust her. Do not worry about whether she's going to leave or not, all you need to do is to be the best version of yourself. You may feel hurt at heart now, but thirty and fifty years later when you look back to remember this day and all the ladies that have left you, you will be happy they did—because you now have a very beautiful and amazing wife who loves you till the end. Then you will understand that you weren't the one with the problem, they were.

Anger does more harm. It drives out many very important factors needed to have a happy and successful relationship like communication, trust, peace, fun, happiness, respect, deep connection, love and intimacy.

From nagging and criticism to physical and verbal abuse, you must deal with this hurtful issue. Yes, it can be very difficult to overcome, but it's possible and only when you recognize the real problem that has accumulated anger inside you, and communicate with your partner, will you overcome it. Do not be shy or scared to share it with your partner, the more you try to keep it within yourself and fight it alone, the deeper it consumes you. You've got nothing to lose by sharing it with your partner, but have everything to gain. Think about your relationship and how much you want it to work; let that drive your will to overcome the real enemy. Try to be conscious of those things that often get you very angry and work hard to not make them become an issue for you again. Whenever you feel your pressure rising into anger, try counting from one hundred backwards. Remind yourself of your decision to not let your feelings control you anymore. The more aware you become of it, the easier it is for you to finally gain control.

Keys to a Woman's Heart

Chapter 7

Communication

A major reason marriages drift apart is the inability to communicate properly and effectively between couples.

At the beginning of relationships, we talk and give of ourselves, generously and abundantly. But talking intimately is a learning curve for most of us and once we move past the honeymoon phase where we want to be so deeply connected we're almost inside each other's heads, the spontaneous impulse to connect intimately lessens or even disappears.

It's hugely important that you communicate well with each other. For how can you know each other if you don't tell each other who you are? How can you know each other if you both don't clearly communicate what you're thinking and how you're feeling? We often forget and change and stubbornly like to think we know everything, but perhaps we don't. We need to keep sharing information about ourselves throughout our time together and throughout our lives, so that we know who we are today.

We need to choose to talk and let each other in on how we're feeling and what's going on in our lives concerning our current ideas, aspirations, ambitions, and aims.

It is of course quite to get by a relationship without talking much personally. But for the active, thriving happiness that you're seeking it is very important to know each other. Anything less is a mirage.

Communicate is a vital aspect of every relationship. It creates understanding and builds stronger intimacy, deeper connection, and love between two couples.

Mutual understanding is the essence of a relationship. As you relate to each other intentionally and meaningfully, you engage and involve each other in your individual lives and your life together, and actively participate in the love you constantly look after and renew.

Consider the ways in which you share information about yourself with your partner. Talking is usually the major channel for our thoughts and feelings. But do you talk to each other as you used to? Do you generously share your current ideas and feelings while listening to hers? Is it a habit you've lost in the hustle and bustle of work, family, leisure activities, and looking after your friendships? Maybe, you are watching what to say to avoid offending her, which is sensible but can go too far—many get so good at not saying what they want that in the end, they lose the art of openness and honesty. But all it takes is a willingness to practice talking—really politely and meaningfully talking—again with your partner.

So agree to practice. She will almost certainly be glad that you want to. Help each other, remember that conversation is like tennis—you take turns. Learn to communicate your feelings with her. Let her know often, what you think, how you actually feel, and what you expect at each occasion.

Learn also, to listen to her when she talks. Listening is the single most important communication skill as it is the best way to understand her. A good listener does more than just hear words; they interpret emotions, behaviors and respond appropriately.

Learn to give her a chance to share her own ideas and view with you in every situation. Giving her a chance to talk and listening gives her a feeling that she is as important to and you respect her very much.

Chapter 8

Keep Up Connection and Love

Have you ever had a time when you felt really close and connected with your partner —a time when you felt emotionally intimate with her? A time when you felt light and playful with your partner? Or a time when laughter flowed easily? A time when you felt like telling your partner your deepest secret and it would be accepted?

We all yearn for a deeper connection with our partner, yet just a few couples seem to be able to maintain the emotional intimacy for a lifetime. Most of our relationships are not very deep, even if they appear to be. Most of us may love our partner very much, but are still not connected at the deepest level. We can have lovers with whom we've shared a passion, profound intimacy, and the sense of a connection with --and then for one reason or another, drift apart. And years

71

later when you meet your former lover, you may have a strange shallow sensation of there being literally no connection anymore.

This is a common experience for most people. But how can such a thing be? How can we claim to love someone so deeply and then find the love and connection to be gone, nowhere to be found?

But what could make a couple feel disconnected?

In the beginning of a relationship, we live more in the present moment. We learn to appreciate our partner, very eager to know each other deeper and totally enjoy each other's company. But, after we get used to that person, we begin to live more in our heads.

Instead of experiencing our relationship, we start experiencing our thoughts on the relationship and our partner.

We build the feeling that we already know everything about our partner, and we take them for granted.

Instead of listening to our partner, we make our own assumptions about them and what they're telling us. We fail to listen and we do not realize that we're living through our thoughts and not the real relationship.

What Deep Connection Actually Means

Victoria Erickson, the author of *The* Edge of Wonder, remarked, "When connections are real, they simply never die. They can be buried or ignored or walked away from, but never broken. If you've deeply resonated with another person, the connection remains despite any distance, time, situation, lack of presence, or circumstance..." American clinical psychologist John Welwood observed, "A soul connection is a resonance between two people who respond to the essential beauty of each other's individual natures, behind their facades, and who connect on this deeper level. This kind of mutual recognition provides the catalyst for potent alchemy. It is a sacred alliance whose purpose is to help both partners discover and realize their deepest potentials. While a heart connection lets us appreciate those we love just as they are, a soul connection opens up a further dimension—seeing and loving them for who they could be, and for who we could become under their influence. This means recognizing that we both have an important part to play in helping each other become fully who we are . . . a soul connection not only inspires us to expand but also forces us to confront whatever stands in the way of that expansion." Perhaps we would be better off if we took the words of Beau Taplin, who said, "Once a deep and powerful connection between two people has been made they become a vital part of each other's lives and there is no separating them. No measure of distance or duration of silence can prevent the outbreak of smiles and laughter or the strong desire to leap into each other's arms when they come together once more."

The problem is that most men do not understand what it means to become deeply connected to their partner. They only understand it in the aspect of sexual satisfaction and the lingering in the bed. To be connected to your partner is to share the same thoughts, goals and vision with her. It is to be connected emotionally, psychologically, mentally, physically and spiritually with your partner—to always yearn for each other's warmth. To share your every thought, dream, goal and your whole life with the other.

Distance can never be a barrier to a successful relationship when there is a deep connection between two lovers. Most of the time, there are often the problems of distrust and the loss of deeper love when one partner gets to move away because of school or business. When your partner moves, you begin to wonder most of the time what she may be doing at a particular point in time or who she's with at the moment. You lose your trust and love for her because you think she may have lost hers too. But most men are often disappointed when they hear a knock at their front door and only to realize that their partner never lost theirs all that time.

Intimacy isn't purely physical—it's the act of connecting with your partner so deeply that you feel like you see into their soul.

A deep connection brings deeper feelings that even when you both are not together, physically, sharing the same time and space, you can feel her presence and warmth almost as when she's with you, and you love her even more that no other lady interests you.

It's that which cements two lovers together cohesively making their love last a lifetime. You may have lost the connection with your partner, but you can build it back—its never too late.

How to Connect/Reconnect With Your Partner

Spend Time Together.

You cannot build a deeper love and connection if you don't spend quality time with your partner. Time is fundamental to building a stronger connection and achieving a lasting relationship.

Addiction is the practice of an attitude over a long period of time. It doesn't happen in one day or one week. It's a continuous practice. The more time you spend practicing an act, the more addicted you become to it.

A relationship is exactly the same. The more quality time you spend with your partner, the more addicted you become to her and the more you build a strong emotional connection.

It is a continuous practice, not for a short time. Do not say that you know your partner well now and need not spend more time with her. Learn to share your thoughts and feelings with your partner every now and then.

People develop new thoughts and feelings each day; this means that no matter how much you think you know your partner, there are always new things to learn about them. You never stop learning until you die.

If we understand the special connection between some mothers and their sons, as awkward as it may seem, they never got so close in a day or a year. It literally took more than half the man's life. Spending time together creates room for you and your partner to share and learn new things about each other. Oscar award winner David Niven said, "Never stop learning and adapting, the world (your partner and relationship) will always be changing. If you limit yourself to what you knew and what you were comfortable with earlier in your life, you will grow increasingly frustrated with your surroundings as you age. Or perhaps, if I adopt the wise words of Warren Buffet, "It takes twenty years and more to build a great relationship and five minutes to ruin it. if you think about that, you'll do things differently."

The more quality time you spend and share with your partner, the more emotionally connected you will become and the more successful your relationship will be.

Building Trust.

 Learning to trust your partner starts by first, trusting yourself. Accepting yourself for who you are.

Some men always think the negative when their partner is out to visit a friend or for work and they are quick at doubting their partner's feelings for them. There are two reasons for such distrust. Either because they do not see themselves worthy of their partner and so are always scared that there may lose her or because they're actually unfaithful to their partner and so they think that their partner is doing the same—they don't trust their partner since they do not trust themselves. Either way, you can feel the connection between the both of you drifting apart.

You have to accept yourself for who you are. You must understand that no one is perfect, and so you can never be, but as far as you keep improving yourself, she is that way too and if she didn't find you worthy, she wouldn't have accepted your proposal.

There are some unreasonable decisions that go along with the thought of not being worthy of your partner. You may start monitoring her actions or to an extreme banning her from making friends. Acting these ways will only sour your relationship and drift you both apart.

Grow your self-esteem. Know your worth and learn to trust your partner and respect her personal life.

If you've been unfaithful, then you have to stop. Ask yourself, "What am I searching for another woman that my partner does not have or cannot give me?"

It's very disappointing to see some men abandon the gold they have to chase after stone. You leave your partner for some lady at your office or some other place for some reasons too that seem stupid.

You absolutely do not have any reason whatsoever to cheat on your partner, no reason. And if there is something you long for in that other lady which you can't find in your partner, why not make her become that? If a woman truly loves you she will do anything to please you. It's in their nature.

As far as you remain unfaithful the connection will always drift apart. You wish to build a deeper connection with your partner you have to decide now to stop. Work, learn and grow together with your partner. It's not so difficult; you start with a true decision—to stop cheating. There's nothing that drifts two lovers apart like infidelity.

You can build a deeper connection with your partner if you learn to trust yourself as a very faithful lover and trust your partner that they are too.

Honesty

Honesty is a very vital key to building a deeper connection and love. Constantly communicating with your partner about what you're thinking and how you feel and any given time brings about learning and understanding the other. Discuss with them about whatever you feel that they're doing that you don't actually appreciate where you may need them to improve on and you can see her improve. Communication is very important.

Keys to a Woman's Heart

Chapter 9

Keeping Up the Romance

Romance—a heart throbbing, pulse-pounding, tear-jerking desire. It permeates our lives, appeals to our diaries, and tugs on our hearts. It's a spark-plug of our love relationships, an essential element in our psychological well-being. I call it food for the soul. From teen years on into adulthood, we'll yearn for the emotions and excitement of romance. But soon after we're married or in a relationships, we lose it.

Only one in every ten relationships and one in every twenty marriages keep and maintain romance after three years of their courtship.

We are always fond of making excuses—work, kids, too many responsibilities. And day after day relationships continue to break and marriages drift apart because either of the couples no longer enjoy their relationship anymore.

What some men don't know is, though circumstances may have changed—you are now very busy with work, you've got kids, lots of responsibilities, but your relationship hasn't. In fact, keeping and maintaining a romantic relationship is a vital responsibility and necessity.

According to facts, three of every five married couples hate their married life. Most say they feel imprisoned and some say, it's boring and they get frustrated at the end.

This is because they lack the romance in their marriages. They lack the play in their relationship. They've lost the sweetness and now feel like vomiting.

Most men think of sex when they hear the word—romance, but that isn't what it really means. Romance is more than just sex. It's all about emotion. It's the teasing and the flattering. It's having fun together and enjoying each other's company. It's all the playful fights and tinkles. It's more of the kisses and the gentle touches, especially early in the mornings and at night (not sex.) It's the calling from work just to say the three words—I love you. It's attention and surprises. It's desire, empathy, and fantasy. It's that which sparks up all the nerves in your body like an electric charge that makes you want to make love to your partner. It's being in love.

Romance does the work of a sweetener in a soup—a relationship is tasteless without it—boring and without fun. We all need fun in our lives no matter how old we are or how busy we may be. We'll know the saying about Jack that says, "All work and no play make Jack a dull boy."

Ask yourself, when was the last time you bestowed the kind of romantic attention and gestures on your spouse that you bestowed during the early days of your courtship? It's up to you to take the initiative.

No one would disagree that children can be a hindrance to spending quality time alone with your partner, but there is always a room to create romantic atmospheres for you and your partner at least once every month.

The romantic atmosphere would help you get away from the ordinary preoccupations of life, away from children, phones, and vocational concerns and in a new environment concentrated instead on loving each other. Create time to have personal interactions and appreciations and this would definitely increase oneness between the both of you.

The best atmospheres include: dim lights, a cozy winter evening with an open fire, sitting out on a patio or porch in the spring or summer moonlight, sitting out on a couch watching the evening sun as it sets while you both talk about something enjoyable, going out on a date, picnic lunches in a quiet park, strolls through a calm street or beautiful garden holding hands, playing and interacting, exploring even if you do not have a destination, driving around, or spending a night or two together in a hotel. Whatever you do, keep it just for the two of you.

Women are romantic beings. They spend millions every year on romantic novels. Their magazines concentrate more on love romances and other peoples' affairs on how to exercise and dress better to look attractive and have even more romance. And this shows how greatly important romance is to women.

One of the very consistent and important aspects of romance is ***passionate kissing***, but it's tragic to know that more than 60% of married men can't remember the last time they kissed their wife four years after their marriage.

A passionate kiss is the most romantic way to communicate with your partner how you feel about her and how much you truly love her. A single stroke from a passionate kiss releases a thousand words. It conveys **_tenderness, passion, and enthusiasm._** Every time you kiss your partner, you tell her so much about your feelings more than you can say in a year or your whole life.

Kissing does more than express your deepest love and feelings. It builds and maintains very strong connections between two lovers. It's one single act doing a thousand jobs.

My question is, "Why do couples stop kissing each other like they used too a few years after marriage?

It's disappointing to say that more than half of those in marriage don't know about a married life. It's a normal misconception by them that a marriage is so different from a relationship, so romance and kissing isn't necessary anymore. They see marriage as a union of a man and wife, coming together to procreate. It is very important to understand that a marriage is an agreement, a covenant, and a decision between two partners to become one and to express passion and love to each other in a deeper level for the rest of their life. Children are secondary necessities.

It is very important that you maintain a great romantic relationship with your partner in your married life.

Build up a great romance in your relationship. Make it a habit kiss your partner passionately every day from today, until your last breath. Lighten up your marriage. Learn to play together like kids. Make her always feel charges like that of an electric all over her body whenever you touch her. Make her always yearn for you every time. Spoil her with romance.

To Women

Sometimes, women behave immaturely by seeking a break up when they feel bored in their relationship. You share the same responsibility to keep and maintain a romantic relationship with your partner just as he does. Seeking a breakup or needing space isn't the best solution, in fact, it's never a solution.

When you feel that your relationship is lacking the romance, bring it back again. The *us* is more important than you. Sometimes he may have a lot of things running in his head and is very unlikely to realize that the relationship lacks romance, so initiate it.

You too can plan a romantic dinner for the both of you alone. Do not see it as the man's responsibility to do so. A relationship is made up of two people and requires the continuous effort from both people in order to actually work.

Learn how you can always bring your partner's focus back into the relationship when he seems to be off. You have a great gift—seduction, and men always fall for it. Use it right.

There are ways to bring back your partner's focus into your relationship. You could welcome him home from work in a sexy nightgown that fits nicely and makes you look extremely attractive and beautiful. Give him a bit of what you're endowed with and while you both are enjoying yourselves, you can tell him about what you have observed and what you think the relationship needs. This, of course, isn't the only way, there are other romantic ways to get his focus back like preparing his favorite meal or planning a surprise dinner and so on (you know your partner so you know what actually turns him on).

Work together with your partner to build the lasting and romantic relationship you've always wanted.

Chapter 10

Marry Her Each Day

Do you remember when you both walked down the aisle? Do you remember those vows you made to her or have you forgotten them?

Do you also remember how beautiful and gorgeous she looked in her beautiful wedding dress on that very day? Do you think that it was the dress and whole make-up that actually made her extravagantly beautiful? No. It was neither the dress nor the make-up, it was the very moment your heart became one with hers. You have loved her all those times you've been dating, but you felt something stronger which filled your heart and eyes that all you felt and saw in and on her was the radiance of her beauty. You were very happy to begin a journey with your partner, to share everything without anything holding you both back.

Possibly, you may have told your parents that she's the woman you truly love and want to spend the rest of your life with and if you don't marry her, you will die or remain single for the rest of your life.

But what happens then, five, ten years after your marriage? Will you still die for her just as you said before the marriage or was it just a slip of tongue?

Oftentimes, we are so carried away by our own desires, either marriage or anything else that we tend to forget the significance of what we so desire and the promises and vows we made.

Marriage is more than just a union. It is a lifetime commitment and a covenant. The actual marriage itself isn't the whole celebration. Neither are the dresses or the flowers, or the marriage license, or even the children. Do we even know the meaning of the ring we wear on our wedding day?

The one thing that defines our marriage is the vow we made to each other. By marrying and saying those vows, we take an unbreakable oath to each other; the ring is simply a symbol of the oath we took. It is stronger than a blood covenant because while a blood covenant requires blood, marriage requires our hearts and souls.

But unfortunately, most of us don't know what we are doing. You made a vow to your partner to love her, to cherish her, to adore, to take good care of her and to be the best man ever for her every day of your life until you are gone from this world. And this means that it won't end after five years or thirty years, but forever, till death does you part. Truly, what's important isn't what you have said to her on that day you married her, but how much you do your best to live up to your promises every day of your life.

Marry your partner every day you wake. Always feel the kind of energy and love you felt for her the day you put a ring around her finger in marriage. Kiss her as passionately and long just as you kissed her on that very day, each day. Hold her daily as you held her on your wedding day and tell her every day how beautiful, gorgeous, elegant and breathtaking she is, just as you did the day you married her.

Love has no limit. One can never love enough. It's never a static force. It grows every day. It means that each day that comes by, one ought to develop a stronger love for their partner than yesterday.

To achieve a happy and successful relationship with your partner is much more than just wishing for it. You must work for it. It demands your effort and consistency.

You have to start today, not tomorrow. Actions speak louder than words and procrastination is the companion of a lazy man. Every successful relationship and marriage takes continuous effort and hard work from both partners.

You have to set a goal each day in your relationship. Everything is achieved when goals are set. Whether you want to be rich someday, or have your own company, or win the Oscar's. Setting a goal or goals in your relationship and marriage help you make day to day plans on how you can achieve it and it also sets your focus on your goals. Every morning when you wake, say to yourself honestly, I'm going to do my very best to make my partner happy and to strengthen my relationship today, just like you do every morning before you start your day's activities.

Deciding, setting goals, making plans, starting, working hard, being consistent, having faith and believing. Through these steps, success is achieved and is the quality of every successful person. To achieve a happy, long lasting relationship, you also abide by these qualities.

Here are few things that can make a difference in your relationship and marriage:

1. Make a decision to love each other deeply today.

2. Build up.

3. Listen carefully.

4. Greet each other warmly.

5. Apologize humbly.

6. Step away together (have fun).

7. Smile at each other.

8. Kiss each other passionately.

9. Forgive fully.

10. Pray for each other.

11. Appreciate each other.

12. Offer kind words.

13. Believe in each other.

14. Communicate with each other every time.

15. Shrug off small annoyances.

16. Make love to each other always.

17. Be honest.

18. Plan together.

19. Spend time together.

You're in a relationship, act like it.

"Teamwork: simply stated, it is less me and more we."

—LAWMAN Jr.

"Coming together is a beginning; keeping together is progress; working together is success."

—HENRY FORD

Too often, single men who have been dating for a long time and finally find that woman to have a relationship with, continue to act single. They prefer to keep things to themselves, make decisions that require both partners, alone;   to stay out late nights, neither call from work or the gym to say hello. Some even go to the extent of flirting with other girls and say that there is nothing wrong with it. They act as if they're still single and fail to acknowledge the presence of the lady in their life.

To such men, career, friends, and self-satisfaction are much important than their wives and family. They find their relationship or marriage a distraction.

They tend to portray the "good guy' image to the public, but never seem to care about their partner or children.

They portray traits like magical thinking; often saying I want to be rich, without putting real effort into making money.

They are often narcissist. They are extremely selfish, with a grandiose view of their own talents and craving for admiration. They expect their wife or girlfriend to always be available to take care of their needs, without doing the same for her.

They also portray the character of escapism. They often find comfort in addictions, like alcohol and drugs, and even threaten to leave, especially when they encounter stress.

This behavior is the lead contributor to the rampant relationship and marriage break-ups. Men who behave this way unintentionally make their partner feel like she isn't important. You make them feel like you are not letting them in. Some women suffer untold psychological torture and emotional stress, and when it's too much for them, they go for a breakup. And you may begin to wonder what may be the reason.

Every woman wants a mature-thinking man who wouldn't mind sharing his life, time, thoughts and feelings with them. They want a man who is ready to be committed to their relationship and marriage and not act like they (the women) don't matter. They want their man to be their best friend and not just an occasional partner.

True unconditional love is not just about sharing a bed and knowing you always have a companion for dinner. A true lover wants to hear everything, flaws and all. If a woman truly loves you, she would want to spend time with you, be eager to know how your day went, share her thoughts, listen to your dreams, and want to hear your voice all the time. If you have such a woman beside you, you are the luckiest man.

Giving up our "single mindset" is important to a healthy relationship. Transforming from acting single while in a relationship or being a married-bachelor into being a mature man who is truly committed and always acknowledges his significant other, isn't easy, but it is achievable if you want to do it.

First, you must start by acknowledging that you're guilty of the fault and work hard yourself to be the man your partner desires.

Take a Thinking Time

Do I believe that by sharing and working together, you can grow stronger?

Self Assessment:

1. Do I often think more about myself?

_____

_____

_____

_____

_____

_____

_____

2. Do I take my relationship more seriously than anything else?

_____

_____

_____

_____

_____

_____

3. How often do I work together with my partner? Are the times I have decided to work alone much more than those times we have actually worked together?

_____

_____

_____

_____

_____

_____

4. Writing a list of the most important things in your life, where would I place my marriage and family? (be sincere at this).

_____

_____

_____

_____

_____

_____

5. What does my partner think about my method of communication with her? Create a free time and discuss about your relationship with her. Be willing to accept whatsoever her thoughts may be.

_____

_____

_____

_____

_____

_____

_____

_____

_____